DAVID BOWIE.

THE LITTLE BLACK BOOK

"MAY THE WISDOM OF THE GREATEST MINDS BECOME YOURS."
S. C. HOLLISTER

RED POCKET BOOK PUBLISHING

TO DAVID BOWIE,
THANK YOU.

CONTENTS

THE LITTLE BLACK BOOK USED TO BE A MEANS OF GETTING IN TOUCH WITH PEOPLE WHO COULD GIVE YOU WHAT YOU WANTED; MOST FAMOUSLY UNDERSTOOD AS A BOOTY CALL BOOK.

BUT, IN THIS 21ST CENTURY VERSION OF THE LITTLE BLACK BOOK, WISDOM AND KNOWLEDGE ARE THE KEY TO OPENING DOORS.

THIS BOOK CONTAINS 142 QUOTES AND BASICALLY NOTHING ELSE. IT IS UP TO YOU TO DECIDE HOW TO USE THEM. WHETHER YOU READ TO GET TO KNOW MR. BOWIE, OR READ TO LEARN SOMETHING BY EXAMINING AND APPLYING WHAT HE SAID TO YOUR LIFE, WE'RE ALL DIFFERENT.

THE DESIGN OF THIS BOOK INVITES YOU TO MEDITATE ON THE WISDOM WITHIN, HAVE FOCUSED CONVERSATIONS, OR PROTECT YOUR COFFEE TABLE FROM CONDENSATION. WHATEVER YOUR USE FOR THIS BOOK, I HOPE IT DOES SOMETHING TO ENRICH YOUR LIFE; EVEN IF IT'S JUST KEEPING YOUR COFFEE TABLE LOOKING NICE.

MAY THE WISDOM OF SOME OF THE GREATEST, BECOME YOURS.

DAVID BOWIE.

THE LITTLE BLACK BOOK

David's Little Black Book

~

1. I LOVE LIFE VERY MUCH INDEED.

2. I DON'T CARE WHAT ANYBODY SAYS. I LIKE DOING IT AND I SHALL CONTINUE TO DO IT.

3. I FIND THAT I'M A PERSON THAT CAN TAKE ON THE GUISES OF PEOPLE I MEET. I CAN SWITCH ACCENTS WITHIN SECONDS OF MEETING SOMEBODY AND I CAN ADOPT THEIR ACCENT.

4. I'VE ALWAYS FOUND THAT I COLLECT; I'M A COLLECTOR. I'VE ALWAYS JUST SEEMED TO COLLECT PERSONALITIES, IDEAS.

5. I HAVE A HODGEPODGE PHILOSOPHY WHICH REALLY IS VERY MINIMAL.

6. I BELIEVE IN AN ENERGY FORM. I WOULDN'T LIKE TO PUT A NAME TO IT.

7. I SEEM TO DRAW A LOT OF FANTASIES OUT OF PEOPLE, ALL THE FAN MAIL I GET. A LOT OF IT IS AWFULLY NICE, 'HOW'S YOUR BABY? HOW'S YOUR WIFE? WHAT'S YOUR MUM'S NAME?' SOME OF THEM ARE WORTH FRAMING.

8. I'M WRITING A NOVEL BASED ON THE TRANS-SYBERIAN EXPRESS.

9. SHE WAS AN INTELLECTUAL THAT WENT TO SCHOOL IN SWITZERLAND AND HAS A VAST CAPACITY FOR KNOWLEDGE. RUNS AROUND AND DOES THESISES ON EVERYTHING.

10. THERE'S NOTHING REALLY TO UNDERSTAND. I'M A STORY TELLER,

AND A STORY WRITER AND I
DECIDED TO ENACT A LOT OF THE
MATERIAL I WAS WRITING AND
PERFORM IT AS MYSELF AT THIS
MOMENT.

11. NOTHING THAT I DO IS ON ANY
KIND OF INTELLECTUAL SLANT.

12. I HAVEN'T MADE ANY DECISION
ON IT [TO SAVE HISTORIC HOUSES
FROM BEING TORN DOWN]
BECAUSE I KNOW A LOT OF
FAMILIES THAT NEED HOUSES. AS
MUCH AS I LIKE A LOT OF THE
ARCHITECTURE... I DON'T KNOW.

13. MOTIVATION OF POLITICS? IT'S
FINANCE.

14. I AM A PERSON OF DIVERSE
INTERESTS. I'M NOT REALLY VERY
ACADEMIC BUT I GLIT FROM ONE
THING TO ANOTHER, A LOT.

15.   I SAW THE BOOK AT MICK
      JAGGER'S HOUSE, AND I NICKED
      THE IDEA FOR DOING A COVER.

16.   NOW THAT I'M STANDING THERE
      WITH THE BAND AND JUST
      SINGING MYSELF, I'M FINDING A
      NEW KIND OF FULFILLMENT. I
      WILL GO BACK TO PRODUCTIONS
      BUT I JUST WANTED TO GO OUT
      AND SING MY SONGS AS A SINGER.

17.   I WENT TO A TECHNICAL COLLEGE
      NEAR LONDON... I TOOK ART.

18.   DON'T ASK ME ANY QUESTIONS
      BECAUSE I'LL SAY SOMETHING
      DIFFERENT EVERY TIME.

19.   THE LIVES OF THE ROCK STARS ARE
      REALLY NOT AS STRANGE AS THE
      LIVES OF THE FANS.

20. WHEN I FIRST STARTED, I COULD GET OUT AND ABOUT A BIT. AND I USED TO GO TO CLUBS AND DANCE, YOU KNOW. THAT WAS QUITE EASY. I SORTED OUT WHAT I WANTED TO WEAR AND WHAT I WANTED TO DO. BUT LATER ON WHEN THINGS BECAME SLIGHTLY COCOONED, I FOUND I WAS SEEING WHAT EVERYBODY ELSE WAS WEARING. I USED TO COME TO THE SHOWS AND THOUGHT, 'HM. YOU'RE KIND OF OUT OF IT A BIT.' SO I KIND OF GET INFLUENCED BY PEOPLE THAT COME TO SEE ME.

21. I SAW A PERSON WITH A CANE ONCE. SOMEONE STARTED BRINGING THEM TO THE GIGS, AND I REALLY LIKE THEM SO I STARTED USING ONE. IT WASN'T ME, IT WAS THEM.

22. I'M IN A VERY LUCKY POSITION OF NOT WANTING TO FLY. SO I TOOK A SHIP OR A TRAIN OR SOMETHING. (EXPLAINING WHERE HE GETS HIS IDEAS FROM.)

23. ROCK STARS HAVE VERY TANGLED MINDS. THEY'RE VERY MESSED UP PEOPLE.

24. I DON'T THINK I'M OUTRAGEOUS AT ALL.

25. YOU DON'T MAKE ME A HERO. I KNOW I'M NOT A HERO. IT'S JUST WORK.

26. I DON'T KNOW WHERE YOU READ THAT, BUT THAT'S NOT TRUE.

27. IT'S ALL BABIES AND DIAPER CREAM TODAY.

28. I WRITE SO MANY SONGS, I'VE
    NEVER SURE IF I'M GOING TO
    REMEMBER THE LYRICS.

29. I USED TO BE A TIBETAN
    BUDDHIST, YA KNOW.

30. IT'S BEEN PRETTY WELL RECORDED
    THAT MY FAMILY IS RAMPANTLY,
    WHAT'S THE WORD? I THINK I'M
    NOT SO SURE HOW MUCH OF IT IS
    MADNESS. I THINK THAT THERE'S
    AN AWFUL LOT OF, THERE'S AN
    AWFUL LOT OF EMOTIONAL AND
    SPIRITUAL MUTILATION THAT
    GOES ON IN MY FAMILY.

31. I WANTED TO BE A MUSICIAN
    BECAUSE IT SEEMED REBELLIOUS;
    IT SEEMED SUBVERSIVE.

32. WHEN I WAS A TEENAGER, I
    SINCERELY WANTED TO WRITE

MUSICALS FOR THE WEST END OR
FOR BROADWAY.

33. BOTH MY WIFE AND MYSELF GET
UP BETWEEN FIVE AND SIX IN THE
MORNING.

34. I DIDN'T REALIZE THE ACTUAL
STUDIO WAS AT THE TOP OF AN
EXTREMELY HIGH MOUNTAIN. WE
WERE COMPLETELY ISOLATED
FROM THE REST OF THE AREA. AND
I LOVE THAT BECAUSE I LOVE
ISOLATION AND I'M VERY KIND OF
MASOCHISTIC LIKE THAT. I LOVE
BEING CUT OFF FROM
EVERYTHING. FOR A WRITER IT
JUST WORKED REALLY WELL.

35. I ATTEMPTED TO DO NO MORE
THAN EXPRESS HOW I FELT WITH
THE NEW AGE, MY FAMILY, MY
FEELINGS TO THE UNIVERSE, MY

PLACE IN THIS WORLD AND ALL
THAT. THE LITTLE QUESTIONS.

36. OF THE 26 ALBUMS I'VE MADE, I
    THINK THERE WERE TWO WHERE I
    WASN'T REALLY INVOLVED. THAT
    WAS TONIGHT AND NEVER LET ME
    DOWN. THE TWO FOLLOW-UPS TO
    LET'S DANCE.

37. LET ME JUST EXPLAIN THAT A
    LITTLE FURTHER. I DON'T WANT
    TO GET INTO SOME DEEP SHIT
    HERE.

38. THERE WAS A PERIOD WHEN I WAS
    PERFORMING IN FRONT OF THESE
    HUGE STADIUM CROWDS AND I'M
    THINKING, 'WHAT ARE THESE
    PEOPLE DOING HERE? WHY'D
    THEY COME TO SEE ME? THEY
    SHOULD BE SEEING PHIL COLLINS.'
    THEY WERE DEFINITELY PHIL
    COLLINS TYPE AUDIENCES AND

THEN THAT CAME BACK AT ME
AND I THOUGHT, 'WHAT AM I
DOING HERE? I SHOULD BE
PLAYING TO PEOPLE THAT DON'T
LOOK LIKE THEY'RE COMING TO
SEE PHIL COLLINS.

39. I WAS INCREDIBLY PROMISCUOUS
AND I THINK WE'LL LEAVE IT AT
THAT.

40. THE BLACK NOISE IS THE REGISTER
WITHIN WHICH YOU CAN CRACK A
CITY OR PEOPLE OR UM, IT'S A NEW
CONTROLLED BOMB. IT'S A NOISE
BOMB WHICH CAN DESTROY. WHY
DID YOU ASK ME THAT?

41. WHY WOULD I GO INTO THAT
WHEN I COULD MAKE A FORTUNE
WRITING A BOOK ABOUT IT? WHY
SHOULD I GIVE IT TO YOU FOR
FREE?

42. I'M ALWAYS AMAZED THAT PEOPLE TAKE WHAT I SAY SERIOUSLY. I DON'T EVEN TAKE WHAT I AM SERIOUSLY.

43. THAT'S SUCH A SERIOUS AND LIFE CHALLENGING, AND LIFE CHANGING QUESTION. THE ANSWER THAT I HAVE FOR YOU WOULD PROBABLY CREATE SUCH TURMOIL IN YOUR SOUL, I'M NOT SURE THAT YOU COULD ACTUALLY WITHSTAND IT. I'M GOING TO HAVE TO POLITELY AND RELUCTANTLY, NOT ANSWER THAT QUESTION.

44. I DIDN'T KNOW WHAT IT MEANT TO BE IN A REAL DEMOCRACY UNTIL I KIND OF DEMANDED ONE.

45. MY SON AND I GET ALONG INCREDIBLY WELL. HE'S A WONDERFUL MAN. HE'S GROWN

UP TO BE JUST, BEYOND MY EXPECTATIONS OF WHAT ONE'S OWN CHILD CAN GROW UP TO BE. TERRIFIC, KIND HEARTED, HONEST, STRAIGHT AHEAD; HE'S JUST A GREAT GUY.

46. THE AMAZING THING IS... IT'S AN INCREDIBLE THING; IF I DON'T HAVE THE BOOK WITH ME, I WILL DEFINITELY FORGET THE WORDS. IF I'VE GOT THE BOOK OUT THERE, AS LONG AS IT'S TURNED TO THE RIGHT PAGE, I'LL REMEMBER THE WORDS TO THE SONG THAT I'M DOING. IT'S REALLY ODD.

47. I'VE BEEN UP FOR 29 HOURS. THIS IS ME STRAIGHT, BUDDY. YOU'RE LUCKY YOU DIDN'T KNOW ME 25 YEARS AGO.

48. I HAD A LOT OF FRIENDS. BUT THEY ALL DISAPPEARED WHEN I STOPPED DOING DRUGS.

49. I PAINTED A TULIP. SERIOUSLY. IT WAS DEAD.

50. I PAINTED A DEAD TULIP IN BERMUDA.

51. WE CAN'T WAIT TO BRING OUR SHOW TO YOU. WHATEVER THAT SHOW IS, IT'LL BE FUN. SEE YOU THERE.

52. FOR ME IT REALLY IS ABOUT THE ALBUM ITSELF AND THE CONTENTS OF THE ALBUM, YOU KNOW. IT DOESN'T NECESSARILY, I MEAN, I MEAN I'VE HAD BIG HITS WITH ALBUMS THAT I REALLY DESPISE, FRANKLY. YOU KNOW, ALBUMS I DON'T LIKE. AND THEY'VE DONE REALLY WELL.

53. THE SONGS WERE REALLY MADE TO BE PLAYED LIVE.

54. MY PRESUMPTION IS THAT BECAUSE I'M ENJOYING WHAT I'M DOING, I BELIEVE IN THE SONGS, THEN THAT ENTHUSIASM WILL PASS OVER INTO THE AUDIENCE AS WELL, AND THEY'LL PICK UP ON THAT. SO IT BECOMES A TWO WAY AVENUE, MAN.

55. YOU'VE GOT TO GO ON KNOWING YOU'RE GOING TO HAVE A GREAT TIME.

56. COCAINE WRECKED ME.

57. I DO FALL IN LOVE QUITE QUICKLY. ONCE UPON A TIME I USED TO FALL IN LOVE QUITE A LOT.

58. I WENT TO LOS ANGELES AND I
    LIVED THERE FOR A COUPLE OF
    YEARS. WHICH IS A CITY I REALLY
    DETEST… SO I WENT TO LIVE
    THERE, AMONG PEOPLE I DIDN'T
    LIKE VERY MUCH, TO SEE WHAT
    WOULD HAPPEN TO MY WRITING…
    IT'S A BLISTER ON THE BACKSIDE
    OF HUMANITY, REALLY. DETROIT
    HAS REAL PEOPLE TRYING TO
    SURVIVE. BUT IN LOS ANGELES, IT'S
    FABRICATION IN REAL LIFE.

59. I ALWAYS HAD A REPULSIVE NEED
    TO BE SOMETHING MORE THAN
    HUMAN. I FELT VERY PUNY AS A
    HUMAN. I THOUGHT, 'FUCK THAT.
    I WANT TO BE SUPERHUMAN.'

60. I'M AN INSTANT STAR. JUST ADD
    WATER AND STIR.

61. THE TRUTH OF COURSE IS THAT
    THERE IS NO JOURNEY. WE ARE

ARRIVING AND DEPARTING ALL AT
THE SAME TIME.

62. FRANKLY, I MEAN, SOMETIMES THE
INTERPRETATIONS I'VE SEEN ON
SOME OF THE SONGS THAT I'VE
WRITTEN ARE A LOT MORE
INTERESTING THAN THE INPUT
THAT I PUT IN.

63. I'M NOT A PROPHET OR A STONE
AGED MAN, JUST A MORTAL WITH
POTENTIAL OF A SUPERMAN. I'M
LIVING ON.

64. TO NOT BE MODEST ABOUT IT,
YOU'LL FIND THAT WITH ONLY A
COUPLE OF EXCEPTIONS, MOST OF
THE MUSICIANS THAT I'VE
WORKED WITH HAVE DONE THEIR
BEST WORK BY FAR WITH ME.

65. TOMORROW BELONGS TO THOSE
WHO CAN HEAR IT COMING.

66. THE GREATEST THING YOU'LL EVER LEARN IS JUST TO LOVE AND BE LOVED IN RETURN.

67. TALKING ABOUT ART IS LIKE DANCING ABOUT ARCHITECTURE.

68. CONFRONT A CORPSE AT LEAST ONCE. THE ABSOLUTE ABSENCE OF LIFE IS THE MOST DISTURBING AND CHALLENGING CONFRONTATION YOU WILL EVER HAVE.

69. IF I FEEL COMFORTABLE WITH WHAT I'M DOING, SOMETHING'S WRONG.

70. NEVER LOOK BACK. WALK TALL. ACT FINE.

71. SOMETIMES I'M USEFUL CURRENCY.

72. AND THESE CHILDREN THAT YOU
    SPIT ON AS THEY TRY TO CHANGE
    THEIR WORLDS ARE IMMUNE TO
    YOUR CONSULTATIONS. THEY'RE
    QUITE AWARE OF WHAT THEY'RE
    GOING THROUGH.

73. ALL ART IS UNSTABLE. ITS
    MEANING IS NOT NECESSARILY
    THAT IMPLIED BY THE AUTHOR.
    THERE IS NO AUTHORITATIVE
    VOICE. THERE ARE ONLY MULTIPLE
    READINGS.

74. I WAS BACK IN NEW YORK A
    COUPLE OF MONTHS LATER IN
    SOHO, DOWNTOWN, AND A VOICE
    PIPES UP IN MY EAR, 'ARE YOU
    DAVID BOWIE?' AND I SAID, 'NO,
    BUT I WISH I HAD HIS MONEY.'
    'YOU LYING BASTARD. YOU WISH
    YOU HAD MY MONEY.' IT WAS
    JOHN LENNON.

75. I HAD TO RESIGN MYSELF, MANY YEARS AGO, THAT I'M NOT TOO ARTICULATE WHEN IT COMES TO EXPLAINING HOW I FEEL ABOUT THINGS. BUT MY MUSIC DOES IT FOR ME, IT REALLY DOES.

76. WHAT I LIKE MY MUSIC TO DO TO ME IS AWAKEN THE GHOSTS INSIDE OF ME. NOT THE DEMONS, YOU UNDERSTAND, BUT THE GHOSTS.

77. SPEAK IN EXTREMES. IT'LL SAVE YOU TIME.

78. FUNK? I DON'T THINK I HAVE ANYTHING TO DO WITH FUNK. I'VE NEVER CONSIDERED MYSELF FUNKY.

79. YOU CAN NEITHER WIN NOR LOSE IF YOU DON'T RUN THE RACE.

80. I BELIEVE THAT I OFTEN BRING OUT THE BEST IN SOMEBODY'S TALENTS.

81. DON'T YOU LOVE THE OXFORD DICTIONARY? WHEN I FIRST READ IT, I THOUGHT IT WAS A REALLY, REALLY LONG POEM ABOUT EVERYTHING.

82. I FELT I REALLY WANTED TO BACK OFF FROM MUSIC COMPLETELY AND JUST WORK WITHIN THE VISUAL ARTS IN SOME WAY.

83. YOU WOULD THINK THAT A ROCK STAR BEING MARRIED TO A SUPERMODEL WOULD BE ONE OF THE GREATEST THINGS IN THE WORLD. IT IS.

84. AS YOU GET OLDER, THE QUESTIONS COME DOWN TO ABOUT TWO OR THREE. HOW

LONG? AND WHAT DO I DO WITH
THE TIME I'VE GOT LEFT?

85. I'M PRETTY GOOD WITH
COLLABORATIVE THINKING. I
WORK WELL WITH OTHER PEOPLE.

86. THE MOMENT YOU KNOW YOU
KNOW.

87. IT AMAZES ME SOMETIMES THAT
EVEN INTELLIGENT PEOPLE WILL
ANALYZE A SITUATION OR MAKE A
JUDGMENT AFTER ONLY
RECOGNIZING THE STANDARD OR
TRADITIONAL STRUCTURE OF A
PIECE.

88. I'M A WRITER... I REALLY
WOULDN'T LIKE TO MAKE SINGING
A FULL-TIME OCCUPATION.

89. I SUPPOSE FOR ME AS AN ARTIST,
IT WASN'T ALWAYS JUST ABOUT

EXPRESSING MY WORK; I REALLY
WANTED, MORE THAN ANYTHING
ELSE, TO CONTRIBUTE IN SOME
WAY TO THE CULTURE I WAS
LIVING IN.

90.   I WANTED TO PROVE THE
      SUSTAINING POWER OF MUSIC.

91.   I NEVER RESPOND WELL TO
      ENTRENCHED NEGATIVE
      THINKING.

92.   I WAS PASSIONATELY IN LOVE
      WITH THE WRITING OF SYD
      BARRETT, FROM PINK FLOYD.
      THERE WAS SOMETHING SLIGHTLY
      NOT-QUITE-WITH-US ABOUT SYD
      THAT REALLY APPEALED TO ME
      STRONGLY. THERE WAS A PETER
      PAN QUALITY ABOUT HIM.

93.   WHEN I'M STUCK FOR A CLOSING
      TO A LYRIC, I WILL DRAG OUT MY

LAST RESORT: OVERWHELMING
ILLOGIC.

94. FAME ITSELF... DOESN'T REALLY
AFFORD YOU ANYTHING MORE
THAN A GOOD SEAT IN A
RESTAURANT.

95. I'M JUST AN INDIVIDUAL WHO
DOESN'T FEEL THAT I NEED TO
HAVE SOMEBODY QUALIFY MY
WORK IN ANY PARTICULAR WAY.
I'M WORKING FOR ME.

96. YOU KNOW, WHAT I DO IS NOT
TERRIBLY INTELLECTUAL. I'M A POP
SINGER FOR CHRIST'S SAKE.

97. I WAS VIRTUALLY TRYING
ANYTHING... AND I THINK I HAVE
DONE JUST ABOUT EVERYTHING
THAT IT'S POSSIBLE TO DO –
EXCEPT REALLY DANGEROUS
THINGS, LIKE BEING AN EXPLORER.

BUT ANYTHING THAT WESTERN
CULTURE HAS TO OFFER – I'VE PUT
MYSELF THROUGH IT.

98. MAKE THE BEST OF EVERY
MOMENT.

99. I DON'T KNOW HOW MANY TIMES
SOMEONE HAS COME UP TO ME
AND SAID, 'HEY, LET'S DANCE!'

100. ALL MY BIG MISTAKES ARE WHEN I
TRY TO SECOND-GUESS OR PLEASE
AN AUDIENCE. MY WORK IS
ALWAYS STRONGER WHEN I GET
VERY SELFISH ABOUT IT.

101. I THINK WE ALL LIKE LONG HAIR
AND WE DON'T SEE WHY OTHER
PEOPLE SHOULD PERSECUTE US
BECAUSE OF IT.

102. WE SPENT ENDLESS HOURS
TALKING ABOUT FAME, AND WHAT

IT'S LIKE NOT HAVING A LIFE OF YOUR OWN ANYMORE. HOW MUCH YOU WANT TO BE KNOWN BEFORE YOU ARE, AND THEN WHEN YOU ARE, HOW MUCH YOU WANT THE REVERSE.

103. I FEEL THAT I'VE CONSISTENTLY WRITTEN ABOUT THE SAME SUBJECTS FOR 35, NEARLY 40 YEARS. THERE'S REALLY BEEN NO ROOM FOR CHANGE WITH ME. IT'S ALL DESPONDENCY, DESPAIR, FEAR, ISOLATION, ABANDONMENT.

104. MY PERFORMANCES HAVE GOT TO BE THEATRICAL EXPERIENCES FOR ME AS WELL AS FOR THE AUDIENCE.

105. I DON'T WANT TO CLIMB OUT OF MY FANTASIES IN ORDER TO GO UP ON STAGE; I WANT TO TAKE THEM ON STAGE WITH ME.

106. WHAT I DO IS I WRITE MAINLY ABOUT VERY PERSONAL AND RATHER LONELY FEELINGS, AND I EXPLORE THEM IN A DIFFERENT WAY EACH TIME.

107. AS A PERSON, I'M FAIRLY UNCOMPLICATED.

108. I MEAN, MY WHOLE LIFE IS MADE UP OF EXPERIMENTATION, CURIOSITY AND ANYTHING THAT SEEMED AT ALL APPEALING.

109. WE ARE JUST A SPECIES DEPENDENT ON SURVIVAL INSTINCTS, AND THAT'S HOW WE BUILD UP OUR MORALITIES, ABSOLUTES AND TRUTHS.

110. THERE, IN THE CHORDS AND MELODIES, IS EVERYTHING I WANT TO SAY. THE WORDS JUST JOLLY IT ALONG. IT'S ALWAYS BEEN MY WAY

OF EXPRESSING WHAT FOR ME IS
INEXPRESSIBLE BY ANY OTHER
MEANS.

111. I'M IN AWE OF THE UNIVERSE, BUT
I DON'T NECESSARILY BELIEVE
THERE'S AN INTELLIGENCE OR
AGENT BEHIND IT. I DO HAVE A
PASSION FOR THE VISUAL IN
RELIGIOUS RITUALS, THOUGH,
EVEN THOUGH THEY MAY BE
COMPLETELY EMPTY AND BEREFT
OF SUBSTANCE. THE INCENSE IS
POWERFUL AND PROVOCATIVE,
WHETHER BUDDHIST OR
CATHOLIC.

112. I'VE MADE OVER 25 STUDIO
ALBUMS, AND I THINK PROBABLY
I'VE MADE TWO REAL STINKERS IN
MY TIME, AND SOME NOT-BAD
ALBUMS, AND SOME REALLY GOOD
ALBUMS. I'M PROUD OF WHAT I'VE

DONE. IN FACT, IT'S BEEN A GOOD
RIDE.

113. THE HUMANISTS' REPLACEMENT
FOR RELIGION: WORK REALLY
HARD AND SOMEHOW YOU'LL
EITHER SAVE YOURSELF OR YOU'LL
BE IMMORTAL. OF COURSE, THAT'S
A TOTAL JOKE, AND OUR PROGRESS
IS NOTHING. THERE MAY BE
PROGRESS IN TECHNOLOGY BUT
THERE'S NO ETHICAL PROGRESS
WHATSOEVER.

114. I'M VERY AT EASE, AND I LIKE IT. I
NEVER THOUGHT I WOULD BE
SUCH A FAMILY-ORIENTED GUY; I
DIDN'T THINK THAT WAS PART OF
MY MAKEUP. BUT SOMEBODY SAID
THAT AS YOU GET OLDER, YOU
BECOME THE PERSON YOU ALWAYS
SHOULD HAVE BEEN, AND I FEEL
RATHER SURPRISED AT WHO I AM,

BECAUSE I'M ACTUALLY LIKE MY
DAD.

115. QUESTIONING MY SPIRITUAL LIFE
HAS ALWAYS BEEN GERMANE TO
WHAT I WAS WRITING. ALWAYS.
IT'S BECAUSE I'M NOT QUITE AN
ATHEIST AND IT WORRIES ME.
THERE'S THAT LITTLE BIT THAT
HOLDS ON; 'WELL, I'M ALMOST AN
ATHEIST. GIVE ME A COUPLE OF
MONTHS.

116. I THINK IT ALL COMES BACK TO
BEING VERY SELFISH AS AN ARTIST.
I MEAN, I REALLY DO JUST WRITE
AND RECORD WHAT INTERESTS ME
AND I DO APPROACH THE STAGE
SHOWS IN MUCH THE SAME WAY.

117. I DON'T HAVE STYLISTIC LOYALTY.
THAT'S WHY PEOPLE PERCEIVE ME
CHANGING ALL THE TIME. BUT
THERE IS A REAL CONTINUITY IN

MY SUBJECT MATTER. AS AN ARTIST
OF ARTIFICE, I DO BELIEVE I HAVE
MORE INTEGRITY THAN ANY ONE
OF MY CONTEMPORARIES.

118. SOMETIMES YOU STUMBLE ACROSS
A FEW CHORDS THAT PUT YOU IN
A REFLECTIVE PLACE.

119. I REALIZED THE OTHER DAY THAT
I'VE LIVED IN NEW YORK LONGER
THAN I'VE LIVED ANYWHERE ELSE.
IT'S AMAZING; I AM A NEW
YORKER. IT'S STRANGE; I NEVER
THOUGHT I WOULD BE.

120. FAME CAN TAKE INTERESTING MEN
AND THRUST MEDIOCRITY UP ON
THEM.

121. THERE'S A SCHIZOID STREAK
WITHIN THE FAMILY ANYWAY SO I
DARE SAY THAT I'M AFFECTED BY
THAT. THE MAJORITY OF THE

PEOPLE IN MY FAMILY HAVE BEEN IN SOME KIND OF MENTAL INSTITUTION, AS FOR MY BROTHER, HE DOESN'T WANT TO LEAVE. HE LIKES IT VERY MUCH.

122. I'M WELL PAST THE AGE WHERE I'M ACCEPTABLE. YOU GET TO A CERTAIN AGE AND YOU ARE FORBIDDEN ACCESS. YOU'RE NOT GOING TO GET THE KIND OF COVERAGE THAT YOU WOULD LIKE IN MUSIC MAGAZINES. YOU'RE NOT GOING TO GET PLAYED ON RADIO AND YOU'RE NOT GOING TO GET PLAYED ON TELEVISION. I HAVE TO SURVIVE ON WORD OF MOUTH.

123. ONCE I'VE WRITTEN SOMETHING IT DOES TEND TO RUN AWAY FROM ME. I DON'T SEEM TO HAVE ANY PART OF IT; IT'S NO LONGER MY PIECE OF WRITING.

124. I'VE ALWAYS REGRETTED THAT I NEVER WAS ABLE TO TALK OPENLY WITH MY PARENTS, ESPECIALLY WITH MY FATHER. I'VE HEARD AND READ SO MANY THINGS ABOUT MY FAMILY THAT I CAN NO LONG BELIEVE ANYTHING; EVERY RELATIVE I QUESTION HAS A COMPLETELY DIFFERENT STORY FROM THE LAST.

125. BUT I'VE GOT TO THINK OF MYSELF AS THE LUCKIEST GUY. ROBERT JOHNSON ONLY HAD ONE ALBUM'S WORTH OF WORK AS HIS LEGACY. THAT'S ALL LIFE ALLOWED HIM.

126. I DON'T PROFESS TO HAVE MUSIC AS MY BIG WHEEL AND THERE ARE A NUMBER OF OTHER THINGS AS IMPORTANT TO ME APART FROM MUSIC. THEATRE AND MIME, FOR INSTANCE.

127. WHEN I HEARD LITTLE RICHARD, I MEAN, IT JUST SET MY WORLD ON FIRE.

128. PIXIES AND SONIC YOUTH WERE SO IMPORTANT TO THE EIGHTIES.

129. RADIO IN ENGLAND IS NONEXISTENT. IT'S VERY BAD ENGLISH USE OF A MEDIA SYSTEM, TYPICALLY ENGLISH USE.

130. THERE'S A TERROR IN KNOWING WHAT THE WORLD IS ABOUT.

131. IF IT WORKS, IT'S OUT OF DATE.

132. PEOPLE ARE SO FUCKING DUMB. NOBODY READS ANYMORE, NOBODY GOES OUT AND LOOKS AND EXPLORES THE SOCIETY AND CULTURE THEY WERE BROUGHT UP IN. PEOPLE HAVE ATTENTION SPANS OF FIVE SECONDS AND AS

MUCH DEPTH AS A GLASS OF
WATER.

133. I'M JUST AMAZED HOW FAME IS
BEING POSITED AS THE BE ALL AND
END ALL, AND HOW MANY OF
THESE YOUNG KIDS WHO ARE
BEING FOISTED ON THE PUBLIC
HAVE BEEN TALKED INTO THIS
IDEA THAT ANYTHING NECESSARY
TO BE FAMOUS IS ALL RIGHT. IT'S A
SAD STATE OF AFFAIRS. HOWEVER
ARROGANT AND AMBITIOUS I
THINK WE WERE IN MY
GENERATION, I THINK THE IDEA
WAS THAT IF YOU DO SOMETHING
REALLY GOOD, YOU'LL BECOME
FAMOUS. THE EMPHASIS ON FAME
ITSELF IS SOMETHING NEW. NOW
IT'S, TO BE FAMOUS YOU SHOULD
DO WHAT IT TAKES, WHICH IS NOT
THE SAME THING AT ALL. AND IT
WILL LEAVE MANY OF THEM WITH
THIS EMPTY FEELING.

134. ONCE YOU LOSE THAT SENSE OF WONDER AT BEING ALIVE, YOU'RE PRETTY MUCH ON THE WAY OUT.

135. I CAN ASK FOR CIGARETTES IN EVERY LANGUAGE.

136. THIS IS A MAD PLANET; IT'S DOOMED TO MADNESS.

137. STRANGELY, SOME SONGS YOU REALLY DON'T WANT TO WRITE. I DIDN'T LIKE WRITING 'HEATHEN.' THERE WAS SOMETHING SO OMINOUS AND FINAL ABOUT IT. IT WAS EARLY IN THE MORNING, THE SUN WAS RISING AND THROUGH THE WINDOWS I COULD SEE TWO DEER GRAZING DOWN BELOW IN THE FIELD. IN THE DISTANCE A CAR WAS DRIVING SLOWLY PAST THE RESERVOIR AND THESE WORDS WERE JUST STREAMING OUT AND THERE WERE TEARS

RUNNING DOWN MY FACE. BUT I COULDN'T STOP, THEY JUST FLEW OUT. IT'S AN ODD FEELING, LIKE SOMETHING ELSE IS GUIDING YOU, ALTHOUGH FORCING YOUR HAND IS MORE LIKE IT.

138. MY BROTHER WAS ONE OF THE BIGGER INFLUENCES IN MY LIFE, IN AS MUCH AS HE TOLD ME I DIDN'T HAVE TO READ THE CHOICE OF BOOKS THAT I WAS RECOMMENDED AT SCHOOL, AND THAT I COULD GO OUT TO THE LIBRARY AND GO AND CHOOSE MY OWN, AND SORT OF INTRODUCED ME TO AUTHORS THAT I WOULDN'T HAVE READ, PROBABLY. YOU KNOW, THE USUAL THINGS LIKE THE JACK KEROUACS, THE GINSBERGS, THE E.E. CUMMINGS AND STUFF.

139. I DON'T SEE WHAT'S SO DERISIVE ABOUT TEENY-BOPPERS. AS FAR AS I WAS CONCERNED, THE MIND WAS AT A MOST ACTIVE STAGE AT THE AGE OF ABOUT 14.

140. AS AN ARTIST, I WAS NEVER INTERESTED IN DEVELOPING AND HAVING A CONTINUUM IN STYLE. FOR ME, STYLE WAS JUST SOMETHING TO USE. IT DIDN'T MATTER TO ME IF IT WAS HARD ROCK OR PUNK OR WHATEVER; IT WAS WHETHER OR NOT IT SUITED WHAT I WAS TRYING TO SAY AT A PARTICULAR POINT IN TIME. IT HAS ALWAYS BEEN ESSENTIAL TO ME THAT MY PUBLIC PERCEPTION WAS SUCH THAT I'D BE LEFT FREE TO KIND OF FLOAT FROM ONE THING TO ANOTHER.

141. WHEN YOU'RE YOUNG, YOU'RE STILL "BECOMING." NOW AT MY

AGE, I AM MORE CONCERNED WITH "BEING." AND NOT TOO LONG FROM NOW, I'LL BE DRIVEN BY "SURVIVING," I'M SURE. I KIND OF MISS THAT "BECOMING" STAGE, AS MOST TIMES YOU REALLY DON'T KNOW WHAT'S AROUND THE CORNER. NOW, OF COURSE, I'VE KIND OF KNOCKED ON THE DOOR AND HEARD A MUFFLED ANSWER. NEVERTHELESS, I STILL DON'T KNOW WHAT THE VOICE IS SAYING, OR EVEN WHAT LANGUAGE IT'S IN.

142. THANK YOU.

...

MORE TITLES IN THE LITTLE BLACK BOOK SERIES:

ALBERT EINSTEIN
ARISTOTLE
BENJAMIN FRANKLIN
BILL GATES
BRUCE LEE
DALE CARNEGIE
ELON MUSK
HELEN KELLER
JOHNNY DEPP
MAHATMA GANDHI
MARK TWAIN
MARTIN LUTHER KING JUNIOR
OPRAH WINFREY
RALPH WALDO EMERSON
RICHARD BRANSON
SOCRATES
STEPHEN HAWKING
STEVE JOBS

IF THERE IS SOMEONE YOU'D LIKE TO SEE ADDED
TO THE LITTLE BLACK BOOK SERIES, YOU CAN
CONTACT HOLLISTER ON FACEBOOK AT
WWW.FACEBOOK.COM/SCHOLLISTER OR CONTACT
US AT WWW.REDPOCKETBOOKPUBLISHING.COM

44155228R00033

Made in the USA
San Bernardino, CA
07 January 2017